Stamen

and

Whirlwind

Poetry by Zan Agzigian

Gribble Press
Spokane, Washington

Gribble Press
PO Box 10307
Spokane, WA 99209-0307
www.greymaredit.com

Iris Gribble-Neal, Editor and Publisher
Tom Gribble, Managing Editor

Neal Hallgarth and Katie Garbutt, Cover
Katie Garbutt, Logo on Back Cover
Norvel L. Trosst, Author's Photo

Cover Photo: "India," by Norvel L. Trosst, from the series "Industrial Outback: Variegated Views." Photo taken in 1983.

Special thanks to Dennis Held for his careful and excellent editing.

All Rights Reserved
Zan Agzigian
2008

ISBN: 978-0-9820736-0-5

DEDICATION

*For My Parents,
William James and Dorothy Rose Deery
Loving, Inspirational Forces in My Life*

Roger Dunsmore, *Finalist, Montana Poet Laureate; Professor Emeritus, University of Montana*

"Zan Agzigian has written sizzling poems that burn with deep, painful affections for her family members, Armenian and Irish in Philadelphia, the Bronx, with the scars from a Catholic upbringing—'Catholicism bombed us with her deadliest weapon—the nun...caught us inside our music...' but also with the right compassion for 'cross-eyed Eddie crushing Owl cigars into the bottom of the grind,' for Indians on the streets of Spokane or at the Old Agency of the Flathead Reservation, for unknown soldiers destroyed by our government's war machinery. She rants brilliantly against the appropriation of everything bright and beautiful by obscene capitalist media, and writes the best love-gone-south poem I've read: 'This room is dead with sex'. Don't miss this first book of poems by a brave, outrageous writer: 'I am a saint bitch slave whore/ on trial for today, a watcher'."

Tom I. Davis, *poet, author of The Little Spokane*

"I love most that vigor and transcendence that sometimes comes striding forth in poetry in good shoes or high boots slamming down a dance step, an urban concrete clatter or a country swing and slide. Zan has this captivating generosity of spirit that takes it all in and loves it. These poems mark wit and clangor, and I love 'em."

Acknowledgements:

"In the Kitchen: Mother's Light" *13th Moon*—SUNY, Albany, NY, 1996

"Alita" *Yellow Silk,* Albany, CA, 1993

"Five Days of Fog" *FOCUS,* Jesuit Volunteer Corp NW Publication, Portland, OR, 1988

"Eve Before the Pascal Moon" *ERGO! The Bumbershoot Literary Magazine,* Seattle, WA, 1990

"The Burning Picture: Bury My Heart" *Jeopardy,* Western Washington University, Spring, 1991

"Missing Parts" (Published as "Parts") *Berkeley Poetry Review*, 1994-95 Issue

Contents

I. **Roots**

*B*lessed John Neumann and the Big Miracle Paintings	7
*N*ight Carousel	9
*T*welve with Father Rowan	12
*F*reshman Sex Education at Archbishop Ryan	14
*C*hadds Ford	16
*M*ore Four Stars	17
*T*he Fullest Fire	20
*I*n the Kitchen: Mother's Light	22
*U*ncle Harry	23
*A*lita	25

II. **Montana**

*P*ow-Wow Montana	29
*R*eservation Losses	35
*E*ve Before the Pascal Moon	37
*F*ive Days of Fog in Mission	39
*W*ild Kingdom: Dixon	40
*T*he Burning Picture: Bury My Heart	42
*F*rostbite on Flathead Lake	43
*M*orning at Old Agency	45

III. Stamen

On the Bus through Oregon	49
Basket-Burdened: Woman at the Well	51
Body and Soul: Spring, Listening to Coltrane	53
Goodbyes	55
Missing Parts	57
Volcanoes	59
Why Do I?	61
Carrying a Canvas, Midnight: Downtown Spokane	63
Living Out the Desert	64

IV. Whirlwind

Whirlwind	69
The Unknown Soldier	71
Trickles	73
Saturday Night Poor Fools	75
Reading *Paris Match*	77
Spokane Homecoming	79
Reincarnation of Peggy Proud	81
October Wind	82
Letter to Dan Berrigan	84
At the Funeral Home with Mr. Swain	86

Stamen

and

Whirlwind

Stamen and Whirlwind

Roots

*"Older
I hear the roots
Snap. The crying
Stopped. Ever since
I have been
Dying
Slowly
From the top."*

--Seamus Deane

Stamen and Whirlwind

Stamen and Whirlwind

Blessed John Neumann
and the Big Miracle Paintings

*S*tained glass Incense
In a Fifth and Girard Street church basement,
We're surrounded by dust and relics:
        Translucent   Transparent   Transcendent.

With hands glued together
Aimed at an undulant ceiling,
        Our *Holy Angels* third grade class
Takes turns in procession past
        The mummy of Blessed John Neumann

        Laid flat and functional as a table--
            A waxen mask of bones and lips
        Glass entrapped
        In Latin Mass.

        He is smeared with spotlights and kisses
In this fluorescent chamber
        Suffering from dull color
As Italian Fishtown women do penance:
Sell souvenirs at counters
        With forgiven acumen.

In a side room, the Miracle Paintings hang
        Where we are forced to believe in resurrection:
        Children wrapped in gauze, arisen miracles.
Confessed sorrows sit on our shoulders,
Mosquitoes needling for blood:

Stamen and Whirlwind

Behave mercifully and my life will have life.
Touch my crotch and I'll burn in hell.
Think other names for God than God and
They'll wash my mouth out with soap.

Aware that *seven* and *heaven* rhyme,
                We are children closer to divine.

Stamen and Whirlwind

Night Carousel
--for my father, William

This tender August calls me back
To carousels and chilly air.
My hand in yours, my small steps slack,
That blue-stone college ring you bared
Boldly exceeded simple things:
My sunburn and my unformed wings.
You were the Educated One
Who showed few laughs but knew still ground.

Beyond your gentle eyes I searched
The high waves, their swollen tease.
The seagulls closed up tight like earth
All past the walls of your tall legs.
Tree shadows fondled the streetlights,
Saw hotel windows up like kites.
Wind blew curtains out: a tension
Cloven by the moon's refraction.

The pier was swift with whooping teens
Who, in new clothes, bummed cigarettes.
At candy stands, your sense was keen
To ways of spending frivolous.
"Want to catch the brass ring?" you asked.
And just like that quick we flew past
Hotel neon, past concessions,
Blurring out those false ambitions.

Stamen and Whirlwind

The Carousel was big, rare birds:
Pink flamingos, their beaks sensual,
And mermaids smiling absurdly.
The man yelled at all, "Use buckles!"
As cautiously the night was loaned,
You reckoned with your choice of throne.
"I'll sit right here. You go on there,"
Placed bets on me, my dotted mare.

As you sat left, on Pegasus,
Beside the ribs of my brood girl,
We shot out fast, my head tossed back.
Your white hair mixed a pepper-snow.
The orchestrina churned its song:
"Teddy Bear's Picnic" on and on.
Dear Father, round and round, I felt
Lost to myself, a lovely melt.

My skimming mind became weightless--
An angel's blend of child-god.
At six, I transcended the coast,
Left my seat as we spun near dropped
From underneath. My hand, a fist,
Reached out, opened up, gave a twist,
And that Brass rose up from a sea
Of lined up silver rings. The trees

Fled through light: Your shining smile
Met my eyes. I laughed with brass-struck
Excitement. The waves crashed while
Your timely bit of Irish luck
Entered my heart like a druid.
Still Blessed   Horses still fluid

Stamen and Whirlwind

Our dreams today combine to win
That brass again, again. Amen.

Stamen and Whirlwind

Twelve with Father Rowan

Father Rowan practiced his golf swing
In Our Lady of Calvary parking lot,
Sending invisible golf balls up to God.

Into the middle of Social Studies
With Mrs. LeGiersh he walked,
Smiled his young priest smile
Like we were his children
And he was our some kind of father.

Toni Ann squirmed like she loved him.
That day, we wanted sex education.
He spared asking if we'd had any,
Or if we knew what the words even meant.

(We didn't.)

Our teacher closed the door fast,
Leaving us alone with one small god.

Father Rowan asked
What no one else ever did.
Toni Ann's anxious hand went up.
"What's French kissing?"

Father Rowan's lips opened dry.
"The polluting of the mouth," he said,
As though those weren't
His own forced words.

Stamen and Whirlwind

The priesthood enslaved him a few more years—
He left and married Sister Ann
And in that time sent his balls to God,
Because those who wrote the rules
Wouldn't ever let him golf
On the real course of life.

Stamen and Whirlwind

**Freshman Sex Education
at Archbishop Ryan**
 --for Su Palermo Carr

The notes we slid down narrow aisles
Stood for plates of food as lean as arrows.
We chewed and shot made-up lives into each other.
Sat defiant, our legs not crossed
In alphabetical order between
Long Slavic last names:
Carpinski, Evanowsky, Tarsiewicz, Zarkowsky.

Sr. Inviolata conducted class: us, love and boys.
A drill sergeant in an orchestra:
Ignorant of the music from our strung
 and bowed instruments:
 Passion, hair and penises,
 Even what would flow:
 Our own vulnerable blood.

We pestered the sound of what was worst:
Her teaching sex and boys,
Or her unshifting speeches; the pitch of her undear voice,
Or just how Catholicism bombed us
With its deadliest weapon: the nun.

What was full-anxious-dumb rolled out our mouths.
She took it into her wide lips
With arms crossed tight across her black dress,
Hands disappearing behind a front flap crucifix,
Stage set for a magic trick.

Stamen and Whirlwind

First she shuffled questions between her feet,
Blackened, kicked them side-to-side: a full deck
Fluttering, selfish, intent on making us forget
What care and bitter boys and men were.

Her awkward body leapt into our awkward bodies
And handled our hearts with a sleight of hand,
Pulled white doves out from catechism one-by-one,
Caught each truth as it tried flying and caged it
At her feet so fast we blinked at what we couldn't see.

Now our scheme was at an end:
A mess: our problems and exploding glands
Leaked out onto patent leather slick linoleum.

Then after: to clean the large lakes up,
On hands and knees in our apprentice uniforms:
Cheerless dark blue jumpers
Entertained in silent laughter and maybe
        dirty underwear.
Where-church-comes-from threats
Piled up rocks of punishment, the feel
That mountains would have if they ever were to die.

Not that she caught us for no real reason but just
That she caught us inside our music, inside the notes
Hot for unspoken pleasure greater
        Than that of our virgin mothers.

Stamen and Whirlwind

Chadds Ford
--for James Wyeth

*I*n search of Venus,
Mud in rough grass,
Roads are train tracks, an elder's back
In paltry winter sun.

Railroad planks,
Counting each one
From rod to nail,
Alderwood to stone.

The leaves clack everywhere.
What's frozen is shining.
Dry cornstalks, old harvest poltergeist,
      A skeletal field,

Wailing marsh once battleground.
Above the Brandywine, geese split screams,
      Fly South.

Face swollen in puddles mirror shadows.
Pockets full of cold fingers.

Over brambles, light disperses
On berries dried up, black and webbed.

Stamen and Whirlwind

More Four Stars
    --for Tadhg and Jim

My faery-ful Bronx Irish buddies party
    Saturday nights
While I'm stuck in a newsstand
Copping sweaty quarters from rich strangers
For early editions of the
    Sunday *New York Times,*
Exposing guts, each bellyful
    "Arts and Entertainment" Section
So I don't have to hear
    People bellyache, *Mine is missing!*

I am Eddie's apprentice. A 45-year paper veteran--
    His training is straight talk:
How old delivery trucks did an honest trade
    On short-order nights like this
When we've already run out of papers:
    Toss an off-shift driver a carton
Of smokes to keep business easy

    As 53rd Street coke traffickers
Pass passed-over-has-been drag queens
    Spilling out of high-class clubs
Even I couldn't afford to be seen in.
    Who covers their sweet asses?

In shameless rain, newly bought french fries
    From the *Big Apple Deli* go limp.
We dodge back and forth between towers of print
    Quickly depleting walls
We've surrounded ourselves with,
    Stopping to sip 2 a.m. coffee
In cold blue cups from the all-night Acropolis.

Stamen and Whirlwind

Eddie swallows a few gulps along.
    With his crossed eyes, people look at him wrong.
I want to detract the look-downs he receives
    From trashed early customers.
Treat me like the idiot
    My straight eyes plead,
I'm the college student.
    Instead, he crushes Owl cigars
    Into the bottom of the grind
That ignorance works hard to put down.
As a reward for humility, he slips himself
A fine cigar kept under wraps at the money stand:
        Smoking the profits up,
He rubs his loose brown-tarred lips,
    Gabs about the *good old days*:
    When New Jersey was struggling before
    The slots rolled into Atlantic City,
        Made it musty and greedy.

Eddie alludes to his daughter:
Her open-heart surgery, bad heart replaced with
    Video Player   Stereo   New TV.

With each tall order, he pulls twine tighter:
    A noose around his neck,
Uses a slipknot he taught me how to make,
    The kind that keeps you from freezing
On the cold street, helps you work faster
    Bundle after bundle, tension
In the length of cigar ashes smearing
    "Sports" Sections.

Stamen and Whirlwind

He takes time to wipe pages off,
    Blames sloppiness on bad eyesight,
Shouts for more four-star finals to wrap.

    When the morning strippers arrive late
    He says, *Know what?*
    Tell ya what I'm gonna do...
And he completes the thankless task of tie and stack
    With the twist of a wavering knot:
        Taut wet at the heart of our chests.

Stamen and Whirlwind

The Fullest Fire
--for my grandfather, Tavit 1890-1951

Tight were those times
What your face was and more
What tugged at your heart
Made you leave
Sinking down
Rising back
Homeland
Old Land

I try to piece together the You
Only free to me in stories
Gentle fragments—fumblings

Your hands polished silver and brass
Your thoughts were soft worries—
Olive-oil fingers
Nails coated with mint and sage
Veins soaked in salt not to forget
What it was not to have

The way you dragged a cigarette
Placed it on a plate
How you sipped thick battles
From small cups of coffee

How every few hours you stared in the dark
Visited by top crosses stone spiral cathedrals
Lamb encircled with dates and pistachios
Blunt rods of rape and revolt

Stamen and Whirlwind

Stories breathe hot
On my soul—
> Create for me
> The fullest fire
> I burn and burn with you
> In this eternal pyre

Stamen and Whirlwind

In the Kitchen: Mother's Light
--for my mother, Dorothy

She gives a special kiss a taste of more:
Saliva smothered lips upon his careening cheek,
A heated slope.

Whose kiss knows best the kiss of flesh on flesh?

She's a bronze Rodin in Philadelphia sun
Crouched circular
Beneath the table.

With pots and pans clanging,
Black beans boiling,
Her man speaking soft bread words,

"Sweet, baby, sweet. You are so sweet."

She's a grey return; a mourning dove
Mounted in silver to tops of spoons
Hidden in parlour drawers.
Sun beams on her belly:
Rolling her dizzy, kissing her crazy
As it enters her.

Whose kiss knows best the kiss of flesh?

For sake of minerals, winter, death,
He swallows her to somewhere dark.
A cave, back into birth and rage.

Brushing the long-lashed air,
Slipping a finger behind her ear,
He drinks, forever swallowing there.

On the floor, she knows what stops.
Lost, what's learned of mother tongue.

Stamen and Whirlwind

Uncle Harry

When my mother tells me over the phone
That all the time your left eye stays open,
(And the one on the right quivers),
I am passed through that open eye
Into your past, into that place I am
Seldom afforded, a venture into the half-soul
Of the Agzigians from Perri,
Into the whole heart of my grandfather.

But now that eye is closed forever.
The one that quivered has ceased for good.
I am shut out from what I do not know,
And weep with open eyes from 3,200 miles
Away from home as my mother tells me so.

"Why" is just another
Unanswered question in a long line of
Questions
Unanswered about my past --
About those places and ancestors destroyed,
About the gift of a gold-filled heart
You gave for my Holy Communion,
About the loss of knowledge.

Godfather: To the gift of gold that once encircled
This small neck, that tickled laughter up
      from my throat,
Memories Tears and Sweat, to all of us torn
From ancestors' beds, their passionate smells
      passed over
By the sun's warmth by torture and death
Somehow polished by grandfathers' hands
In silver and gold, here's a flame
From Sandra--Both Eyes Open--

Stamen and Whirlwind

Long may you linger in the light of form
Unbent unshaped by pinnacles and swords.

I break a hunk of bread in two
And release the body,
Rejoice in descendant tone for what
I've known as you.

Alita

*H*er smile slides as she folds
        Sleeves, clean clothes, the floor
        Disheveled chilled
The room endures Alita

She calls all things that echo Fire:
Rams, and archers,
              Even arrows
                  Until our bodies dive
        To find warm soup

We lick: Our mouths swirl
          Our teeth resist
              The blasting wind

Some old spirits
        (Like old lovers) ride the backs
Of horses loose outside   Hot
Their gallops
        Fog the windows shut

It becomes a house of ice:
            Thighs closed too long
Alita mumbles a word into a pillow
The road she was born on: Killynebber
        We are

Outside breaking puddles in pasture
As hilltops blanket our walk
        Branches sparkle; dogs bark
        And beckon other curs to rise

    . .

Stamen and Whirlwind

    Inside a kettle sweats
Tap Tap crutches wear the old oak floor
      Fire quiets down
Feels crippled Mother over coals
Feed it life with slack, manure

Winter: Cavantown eats late January
      Sips from teacups stained for February
      Winter while wet socks drip
Like spring falls on the mantel

We re-enter
    Send Mother off to bed
    Before she cooks in front of the flames
Leaving me with Alita, the real keeper
Of my doom:

    Lurking inside a witch's womb

Stamen and Whirlwind

Montana

for Victor A. Charlo

Stamen and Whirlwind

Pow-Wow Montana

Come out and play in this highland
Driving that beat-up Mercury of yours
And talk about this Beyond—A reservation,
Where you are Chief and your children
Survive in ancestral meadow tucked and protected
By slanted horse hills that will take me
To Arlee the home of your children that holds
Government-appointed name and not the true
One of Great-Grandfather Charlot.

Along the way you play your insides out
And pass the pipe as moon rises early on Montana
Warm like poetry-stories.   Poets out of time
Begin to sing of sorrow to one another,
Prophesies for tomorrow,
Trying to convince me that I am
My Armenian grandfather's sorceress when really
I'm only a Jesuit Volunteer from the Bronx
For a year playing out my commitment
To my own brand of justice in this place
That makes no sense.

I need you here beside me,
This place's identity. Here it is the 4th of July—
Not your favorite holiday, Indian. We stop at Joe's
        Smoke Ring
For their 9-piece bucket of chicken, the lot crowded
With tourists while the food tips over between us,
But that makes no difference. We are amused
By the White Man's Parade. All we want from today
Is to live to die this time into the ground
Away from Pow-Wow July. How bare and innocent
        I feel

Stamen and Whirlwind

As you talk the talk of chiefs. I'm sure not in the Bronx
Anymore. I hear and see the soft tone hum
Just like the sound of your car engine.
      Here in this meadow
We can make out things the city seems to hide.

"Let's hide!" you say ecstatic for some new destiny.
Screw this 25 mph! Kick up some real moondust
Past the Ole True red-white-blue maxed out at 50,
Down dirt back roads: No cops in sight.
They're all in the thick of the Pow-Wow Kaboom!
Poised outside bars back there waiting for thrill
Of retaliation against Uncivil Warrior Riders,
Don't-Learn-Your-Lesson-Lifers
Who refuse to keep within bounds. *Oh say I can see*
Them as you drive away from *the rockets red glare
the bombs bursting in air* as I pick up a greasy leg
From the carpet, brush it off and bite it laughing
At your string of tease about the Pow-Wow
Heading out while we are heading in--

In hot pursuit of some Larger Wonder
Heading IN---to scout out greater happiness
That can't really be found because it isn't lost.
We aren't lost because we know what we come from
Sets West. You turn east towards Grey Wolf Drive,
Away from the dusk's *early lights* where ranch posts
Look like Coyote if you look hard enough.
"Pull off the road!" I un*proudly hail.* I have dropped
The damn lighter! Pulling off these roads,
      you mumble,
Makes us too obvious in the *twilight's last gleaming.*

Stamen and Whirlwind

Don't want to be so obvious. I feel bad, can tell
The way you stare straight ahead on the lookout
That you are *broad-striped*
        and your eyes are *bright-starred.*
You are so disappointed as I fumble. What a
        worthless scout!

I've lost the fire needed to move out. Chief Shaman Baby,
I have lost your Sacred Light. So what protects your People
Now from this *perilous fight* aka White Man's Mistake?
You and others from you are certain it is
        over the ramparts
And into the Original Reason where the first message
Rose up and was *watched* in dreams
        so gallantly streaming
To grasp the People make them dance give *proof*
Through the night why the dance *was still there*
In the Sacred Circle Pow-Wow Prayer,
        each one a dancer's soul
With no straight lines *oh say* like downtown
Smoke Ring parking lot. That is why
        you wound me through
These Arlee veins.

Does this mean I come up for air past the windshield?
See that *star-spangled banner*ed sky *yet wave*
As the ridge unravels into mountains,
Covers dark clouds *over land of the*se un*free* tribes?
As darkness places shadows on shadows and sheds
Other presences, other patterns across
        *the home of the*se *Brave*
Powers? Our constitution is cracked and you ask quick,
"You done? Put the overhead out." Now everything's
An eagle's glow encroached by cheat weed thistle

Stamen and Whirlwind

Wrapped around barbed wire roads in just one stretch.
It is Coyote who cheats to be thistle, pretends to be cop.
It's a warning that we must watch. I see Coyote.

You say, "Look hard. Just a fence. Don't be
        so easily fooled."
I ask, "What does one say to Coyote if he is spotted?"
Cupped hand holds the pipe, the smoke. You say, "Wait
To see if he has something to say." *Exhale.*
        "Then you take it
From there." I swear there is a better way and you nod,
"Of course, there is, but that's the answer
        you White Folks get."

I huff. What is my consolation? Sitting here I look hard
Into your face as you drive me wild into the color
Of your hair eyes and skin. It is the same as my mother's
Skin when she was young, the same warm tones stirring
On the pages of her 1930s photo album in the scrap heap
Victory Garden smiling for her men at war.
The disappointed look inside her face is your face,
Was that Depression, that same brown-suited dirt
My Aunt Marie calls ethnic ugly. Here it is again.
        All around
The earth seeps from the ground up through this car
Out the roof into this sky. This entire place paints
My existence. And I am sorry, Grandfather,
That you displaced yourself to escape
        the Turkish slaughter.
Sorry you didn't know English, hold its hand,
That face, that job, respect, explain yourself out the door
With a sack on your back and no money for your children.
To be an American.

Stamen and Whirlwind

Chief, don't my ancestor's wails
Take on the same shape as these Arlee hills
Reminding me of songs and stone
        and distant temperatures
I come from? Am I not right feeling the same
        ups and downs
As you from this car out the window? Go ahead and take
The shape of me and hold your shape up. Obvious,
        we are not the same,
But how different really? Somehow that's
        the pursuit we share:
Our Difference as we take it and make it a pursuit
That goes like this:

You tour me through your sacred ground
Just hoping I will understand. Perhaps I will place
        this Arlee
Inside my headheart map into the kind of People I am.
You, Chief, you are the shape of my roots,
        one with hidden powers
Letting me inside where you come from because I am
One of the same. Back there a man lifts a bottle,
Walks without a care. It seems he is moving backwards.

We shoot into your hills away from the bullet-cars.
We change the wind into arrows inside the spirit of buffalo.
You speak of colors, forms, those arrows,
        their feathered noise

Not splintered. You sing the arrows in the wind
        have weight.
You say pray arrows can be read: It is the People's Creed.
The final Consolation we let fly
Up the back of Grey Wolf Drive. I am wondering--

Stamen and Whirlwind

Me, Displaced Daughter, transformed into Carrier of
    Chief's Lighter:
What will I say to Coyote when he says something to me?
I pray I cannot read him nor he me.

Stamen and Whirlwind

Reservation Losses

Out of a second day fog
That brings anticipation on its back
Compacted in the mist
A pressured recognition
Of empty visions
Lines the quarreled streets

Two boys passing on bikes
(One wobbling across the ice)
Come alive and bear
The words in a chill
And damp that quickly spreads

Grandma Woodcock is dead

She was as kitchen window flower curtains
Flutter above the vent
That distills air around my knees
With warm basement breeze

I feel stiff food on dishes
Washing cups and calming fingers
Through fixed and fizzling
        soap bubbles

Ravaged thoughts singled out
        Resting on a death so big
            I shrink
                Into the sink

        Watch an ant swirl
            Down the drain
            Remember some Chief's speech

Stamen and Whirlwind

That no matter how small
Preciousness lingers
On St. Ignatius town

Eve Before the Pascal Moon

*W*e slither through mountains
Heads lost on the back roads
Road signs up, proud and carved
In a day, they'll be covered with gunshot holes

While everything else around
Has not at all a happening sound

In Missoula above *Corky's* voices melt
Ice swimming in warm whiskey
Smearing spots on napkins
High on gin and brandy
The music buzz and poetry
50 miles long

Moonshine after turns the Plains
Into a natural racetrack
Where ghost horses weave
From the high flat plateau
Sewing a full evening together
With red lights of fire and farm towers
At each curve

Chief rides to Great Falls
And I am on his shifting tail
The calls run fast out our windows
And into the river for a pitch
It knows you: the aging hustler
And a crack comes on the edgeless town

Stamen and Whirlwind

I hold this sweet folly: Supernal Sane
In my head   Know the names of thick
                        Map lines but driving on them
Feel they have bodies underneath

We carry years survived in our rhymes
Sided by lakes and shores
Where rocks are polished and soft
You telling me your children's names
           Voice hidden in good medicine wind

Five Days of Fog in Mission

White fog settles on MacDonald Road
       Owl glides through a side trail's throat
Spinning snow from branch
Into thin air
       Ancient faces deep inside green pine
Bed down in ageless dirt
       As sunset's honey hair diffuses last light

A century old cabin is the horizon
       As dry rose petals cradle windowsill
Rolling range: the bison herds hide
       Cows in full view devouring
       Their own silky breath
       Trodding past their troughs of frost
       Twisting tails to trench milk

A cold dog's howl plagues the prairie
Weeds flute tinkle tunes
       Crows perch on abandoned chimneys
Watchful---squawking riot at Mission's
Spread of granite crosses

There is no sky virgins
                     Don't cover with soil

Stamen and Whirlwind

Wild Kingdom: Dixon

We're in our hearts tonight as TV channels flow
Winter howls and fingers thin windows
                Near breaking
The hills outside breathing

We pause at *Wild Kingdom*:
Blindfolded tied moose netted lifted
Swung from his homeland to nowhere

Reservation wind outside sounds
Like the roaring flutter of helicopter
Flying down from outer rim
With undefined ideas in blades
Of displace-kill-off-replace
Unspoken border surprises

We're in our hearts tonight in flowing cold
As TV clips flip images of sixties Indians
When Natives were common and good
While Sunday nights they kept watch
On third packs of Pall Malls:
Redskin-Mutual-of-Omaha
The slaughters silenced to a bitterroot

Inside our hearts still fight
As we pump this small room for sense
All senses awakened from sleep lost in funerals
Butcher-doctor-Indian-hater stories
Hard to hear, to understand
Why men would build crates--
Fence in relentless snow

Stamen and Whirlwind

In your horse-head chair next to tilted lampshade
You drum laughter
Pass-the-bowl-oh-what-the-hell
Keep our grandfathers company
As Penta pours from covert spigots
Operates leftover ringers full of chemicals

Thinking they've got a million years
To destroy what others have been given
Dried-out berry baskets
Behind glass near extinction
Labeled by white men the Wild Kingdom

Stamen and Whirlwind

The Burning Picture: Bury My Heart

The burning picture:
Cheyenne Arapaho White man

With and without hats
Long hair and short
Sweaty brows and dry

Loose bowties and hanging beads

Speaking of nature as Mother
Speaking of expansion as Father

Some at a draw Some in the clear
Rifles clutched
Arrows bows lying straight
Across bare laps

Hands at rest
Arms tight broad backs

Smooth-faced and bearded
Interpreters and hairless poets
Love of war

Also in photo Third from right
The idea of peace...

Not seated, third from right,
An unknown Indian
Someone said he was late

Stamen and Whirlwind

Frostbite on Flathead Lake

     It's a peak day
    Driving Flathead Loop
Shoulder-Blind-Highway
  More what I'm in love with than
        Who I love   Asphalt Absolute
    No doubt in red clay slate

    Used to Seattle gray
    My eyes see shining bark of cherry
    Piled up gray dead as
        Frostbitten
        Grave
        Stone
        Truth

    Certain signs fold over, can't be read
How much can we bear what we don't tell?
    Come here Go there No end
        To osprey coming

What survived spring bite?
The smallest cherries
Hard and sour
Meadow brook and dandelion
Wood to split and free to smoke
Gravel spider windshield cracked
Green orchard window eye shacks
Boarded up

Stamen and Whirlwind

Danger: Texan Tourist
Speeds Impatient
Past Winnebago Warrior
Leaves Town Pump gas truck in the dust
A mad rush to Bigfork to spend fifties
Making meals of Bloody Mary's

Swan Valley cuts wind
Up the strangled river run
Mountains take two minutes
Heartache off our lives
When we look We see like china:
Thin and fragile with a handle

Stamen and Whirlwind

Morning at Old Agency

*I*n summer heat I wake upon
The reservation in a slight cool sweat

Amidst sweet lies,
A full collage of dreams:

That midnight vibrating train
Cow bulls on red clay hills
Then snarls: dogfights 4 a.m.

Awake is less ominous and out the window.
Glittering river turning its power,
Every rapid flows "Good Morning."

The hawks peer down from the apple tree
As I eat cornflakes swallowed with silence.

They know how I fly late mornings,
How in their space I ask solitary questions:

Safe to be restless, somehow hopeful?
(Taloned/Feathered?)

One Pall Mall and I breathe harder, push a broom
Around a corner thinking poems. Cough.

Logging trucks trail awful diesel,
Carry timber: corpses without eyes excreting yellow sap.

When I wake, I smell Pendleton wool burning.
In the sun, I am cautious, think that I am afire.

When I wake up, a towel across my window
Thick with dirt, I think I am invisible as dust.

Stamen and Whirlwind

I sweep up, hear the dead logs roll by
And think that I am one of them.

(There is a God.)

Because I can trace the wasp's nest to the river's belly.
Hear the flutter of wings on flies. Smell my own body.

There's no fooling I've become this place:
Caught up with bison on the edge of scanting pines.

Everything around me orange turning brown:
Tamarack skin peaking at the turn of season.

I am sweeping naked in an Indian man's kitchen
Playing squaw, packing it all in, separating what gets burned

From what gets dumped. I crush empty beer cans
And toss them by the dry elk skulls on lawn.

When I wake up dry skull tight like wind,
I think that I am skeleton, dancing tight in wind.

I am awake, dancing in the deep
Sorrow: this sacred place. So free.

I can pretend I'm only visiting with love.

Stamen and Whirlwind

Stamen

Stamen and Whirlwind

On the Bus Through Oregon

Allowing window breast
Catch glen wind

Crispen sunrise chest
A catacomb

Bombarding silhouette
Of morning

Stark country   dark entry
Thick frost melts

Thin strips of flour foam
Roam the sky

(The brain of glory's head)

Brown bark absorbs
Canyon melodies

(Triptych ties)

Branches ride river to
Mirror forbidden light

A glass-shatter root web

Parted cup of penance
Caped banshee vanishes

In absolute pastures of shadows
Burn bushes   Channel ashes

Stamen and Whirlwind

Chambered grassland:
Rain drowns leaves rustling bent and broken

Frolic mountains (ancient statues)
Coffee weak as heaven

Stamen and Whirlwind

Basket-Burdened: Woman at the Well
--for Mary Frances

*W*ould morning glories trumpet every
Freedom morning up from bondage?
Hear the dawn, a seal unraveling
How I dress the strong plow of the ancients
Dirt rising from the ground?

Could I expose layers of ash, chipped pottery
Underneath the city I walk down to work in?

Let me wear my hair as wide as a house, sweat, yell,
"Come wash me from behind my veil!"
For here, the partitions are too high. No one stops
To glance at mornings other humans
        tan like blended sand.
(Flower buds climb my skin.)

I wish sometimes the disc and horns of Hathor,
The goddess of love, each morning, to be called
Neferetiti at my job, "the beautiful one is come"
With the kind of respect an Arab mother receives.
Instead,
Afraid of Pharoah, ice in my strong eye.

The smells I exhume threaten: Palm, sycamore, fig tree
Jasmine, Crysanthemum, Ointments, Dreams.
The prescriptions my body makes sustain the sun,
Not General Electric, afternoons, is precious as blood,
A daughter of river, (not coffee),
A woman of ribs,
One-millionth in a date forest.

Stamen and Whirlwind

My work makes me Sarah at rest in a cave
Surrounded by statues of gods sitting stony
Awaiting their part on the stage, a new mask
Baking in the sun.

I am not the basket-burdened woman casting spells,
Directing scenes, invisible behind, pouring oils.

Every morning, afternoon I am a saint bitch slave whore
On trial for today, a watcher.
Tomorrow,
       perhaps a bit wiser.

Stamen and Whirlwind

Body and Soul: Spring, Listening to Coltrane

overlooked, the city on this pretty
sun-blind day way up where birds soar
on the eighth floor willing
riesling chilling in the fridge
waiting for the warmth of someone
i dare to ring my borrowed phone.

smoke fills my lungs again.
a cigarette caresses desire
to burst with fullness spilling over.
a guitar lies on its side, my body:
unplayed, slightly warped, the throat
without the heart and guts of it renewed;
a song left hidden unsung intangible,
i unsing my own song.

traffic triples up its form
the streets dance people holding hands.
in alleyways: reflections, puddles.
off the rooftops currents blow some windows,
smiles open. how can it tell what to open
with one tree next to another springing blossoms?
green on green: leaves hugging unpulled curtains:
one house groomed so true with secrets.

heavy bass now penetrates the bay, deep grey with sun
as my hands drum cassettes, keyboard, sweep
a match. another empty smoke. i watch
a squirrel jump chimneys straight across
        the K of C Club roof.

Stamen and Whirlwind

its grey body my grey body jumping careful
soul of city soul of lake the soul of myself, sun:
sprung high and wide extended pairs of pigeons
swoop from eighth floor gutters eight floors down
a parody of body of my soul
one floor that one soul deeper. gone.

Goodbyes
> *--for Mike*

it's like we are a slender country
the way we take walks along each other

lingering in the torrential silence
on top of the torment we take each

other's eyes out one-by-one we bypass each
other's steps in our now too thin apartment

all we do is meet in doorways
but that's not the end of it: we trap words

we are beyond eyes   taciturn
as we think our worst ways to torture

what is left? even when we know we are taking each
other's teeth out from our tender mouths
      that drink the teas

disguise our lips behind crisp toast just to watch each
other swallow crust because this is silence

and now we're just friends on the out
side: loud rain used to be our hands

that held our bodies' dreams like nests
but now what's left? we are these walls

with pictures we put up there: astrology: ourselves:
the recipes of us together evenings

we(were) these hanging keys that open-unlock(ed)
mail--doors--bicycles   and socks?

Stamen and Whirlwind

i'll never roll one inside the other 'til
i'm rescued from a day (another such as this):

songless face this trance-filled dance
of where we aren't gone until we truly go.

Missing Parts

There are still parts
Of me
With parts of you:

Like hands, so far
Gone still in love
Or my lone lip
Now hardening--

Still life: my
Belly rolling empty
Or like what all, but
I can tell:

Like these small words
From nowhere like
A tongue unstuck
Explaining there

In times my eyes
Spread still in love
In lines
To that still part
No name
That tender edge
That is a part of
What is part of you

There move still parts
Of your slim neck
Doctors may have
Names for it but
I don't and

Stamen and Whirlwind

I want all:
That part that name
That still way
Lying there as ordinary
Days   And I endure
My own still parts:
My word   The beat
Hard skipping through
The gone, without you

Stamen and Whirlwind

Volcanoes

*B*lack book spines---*Oceans, Forests, Mountains,*
I choose *Volcanoes* because that's what we were together:
Hot lava bodies with dirt smell of juniper,
Ocean cold, crying waves through a fertile chamber,
Ambitious as the new moon
When it slits itself into an orange slice,
Trails white light fingertips of gas and ash falling to earth.

Our bodies: eruptions, quartz embedded.
Flaming backs grinding into a cliff side.
Inside volcano: inside ourselves,
Ceaseless, slow and primal, lacking water, air:
Rooted islands torn apart, caves with curtains.

These islands: we met like steaming dreams
Pouring a fresh solid landscape.
Our love was panting fire hungry for oxygen.
Not so simple to think about it without hurt:
Beard against my face bursts lost in turning pictures
The old and new of us quivering to a crashing climax,
A shower of red ash piercing our hearts.
My belly a crater, a Pompeii amphitheater
Caved in and covered,
Then silence with the smell of boiling, musty wine.

This room is dead with sex.
Black Alki wind piercing,
No chorus singing through a shallow village crescent
        miles long.
Our lustful volcano is preserved in flat cold pictures.
I have so many just like us upstairs hidden in a box.
The just-like-us hugging mountains in a chain of desire.

Stamen and Whirlwind

Volcano, we are dormant now.
The two of us silent at the throat,
Desiring to spurt through hurried regions:
Furnaces boiling up the banks of men, ready to break
Like the Arc St. Pierre in 1902.

When do you know you're overdue for another eruption?
Your induced state caused an invasion
Of centipedes and ants amid tremors in simple
        peasant yards.
The horses and housemaids ran out into the streets.
Scores of friends became snakes: yellow-brown backs,
        pink bellies
Six feet in length. Their killing bite
Called out soldiers who fought them: 100 lances

Rifle fires crackled more than an hour,
Three days before your eruption.
We need to disturb our alive.
Suddenly the phone is ringing.
I leave history and answer the call
That sounds nothing like you at all.
Rumbling, dull and heatless.
Small: Certainly no one I know.

Why Do I?
--for David Nessen

Because he planted blue morning glories
At the mailbox when he was twelve, right before
His father died and remembers
One of those flowers burst open that very day.
Because he says passed away
Instead of dying when his world
Is shaken up. Yells at the cat
Then feels bad about it.

Because he's full of kid stories:
He rode appaloosas
In the desert outside Salt Lake,
Says that driving
        Flat in the back seat with brothers
        Felt like prison so dull staring up
                At that one and another phone pole.

Took a Schwinn
Up into Draper Canyon
Met a mountain lion:
Either went to church Sundays or pulled up weeds.

When he gets mad he wants to hit
Something, or at least
        Knock it over
        Yet that something is never me.

Because he painted a cougar on the Zoo Bus
        On a fifth of Jack Daniels.
Because he comes from Wapato, and loves the earth,
The Antique Eye who loves to see
        Other people spend money.
Because he can eventually find lost things.

Stamen and Whirlwind

He itches and talks loud when he's drunk, but will shut
Up if someone tells him to stop. He never knows
			what to call
Me and that amuses him. He eats oranges in bed
Late at night and never refills ice cube trays.
Buys cigarettes in bars for quarters.
He loves to do laundry and fold
			Pants in unison with Irish music.
Oh, he hates full moons,
The crazy way they make people want things from him.
Because I know he went to L.A. with a Susan
And he owns jackknives from the Alaskan Expedition.

Because he can be friends with Brianstein
Who thinks UFOs are out to get him,
With a small microchip buried
Deep inside his arm making him forget his mother
Who thinks it's wise to reserve a space
At the UW Bomb Shelter.

Because he gives me opals, taught me
That diamonds are everywhere cold
And not the most beautiful gem in the world.

The clock above his bed is set to his birthdate
And below in his bed
He doesn't sleep there anymore because
He calls me home. Because his dad is Gene
And Barb's his mom. Because he's touched by drums
And swallowtail tattoos. Because he even once
Raised pigs. Because he finds me
When I'm lost. Loses me when I'm too found.
		Just because.

Stamen and Whirlwind

**Carrying a Canvas, Midnight:
Downtown Spokane**
 --for Derek Eliasen

The moon hung flawlessly crowned,
A three-quarter Chihully: A flacon,
Spilling Ode to Midnight down
Upon Sprague Avenue past red fox letters
Towering the sky: A friend stopped,
Switched hands, as we held his oversized
Canvas on the street. The wind

Indiscreet, made his painterly
Forms seem like glass in
The moonlight, gave the illusion the red-
hot reds were sliding to the pavement:
A fiery Fall leaf fluttering
To the grave vase-earth.

Canvas: Moon: Vessel of white,
We held tight, switching hands again,
Resting the tips of the painting on our shoes
(my toes curled) giving amber and yellow
New meaning in the streets.
Art Angels: The Moon, Gabriel
You, Me: Yod en Yod hauling celestial spirals,
Traffic light humming, a-hounding our pace.
We are cyclical, giving ourselves up
After all this work: martyred
By the vast blackboard universe above.

Walking on alone, around a corner after: blue neon
Swims on the window of a Ford. Below
The Spokane River opens its mouth in swirls
To drink whatever illumination life
Has to give, waiting for the hidden warrior to shoot
The stars for one more cup of crystal night.

Stamen and Whirlwind

Living Out the Desert
--for brother, David

I.
Brownes Addition

After two weeks of desert,
Back in Spokane, a valley at the edge
Of desert, Dotson wants
To create a soiled haven
A channel of urban bliss:

an indoor garden,
and brings from our Montgomery Avenue
                           Hot Tomato friend
Four tall stalks of cherry plants
Nestled in four by four bounty boxes
Soft soil with green pepper children
Bursting luscious white buds.

II.
Chesler Park

Fins so old they hurt and moan
And glow with worn white.
Each curve a slickrock path
Slow, unfolding gaps as wide
As teeth falling out: constantly widening its
Solemn mouth. This canyon

Sags like a mother's breasts
Folding gently down, exposing veins
Spreading nipples, eroded bits erected
In a collage before dark.
The downed sun orange and red.

Stamen and Whirlwind

Timeless spread: The Milky Way
Begins to flow from dark
Into a firmly enveloped, thirsty night.

Engrossing path forces us
To be careful not to step
On cryptobiotic delicate black erosion
Eroding from erosion.

The stars
Ask that we put flashlights away --
The desert demands us to
Step, stretch, dance out of ancient,
Ruthless and showering,
Bursting five words for breath
Beneath the bone.

III.
Back Home

First the shirt must come off
For a shallow dive
Into buckets of earth:
Potting soil seven stacks high carried
Over shoulders from three flights down.
We count synchronic steps, 44 of them.
Count endless steps in the desert?
                        Not one of them.

Stamen and Whirlwind

Dotson's back is bad. He can dump the
10-pound bags into this grip and
I'll take them up
Stepping, stretching, trudging out the sweat.

With slow determination,
He loads sacks from
Dad's Buick into, each time, these hands spread,
Awaiting the warm, moist bulge
Of earth. I can't say what it felt like,
Just that it felt like someone.
Mother.

Whirlwind

Stamen and Whirlwind

Stamen and Whirlwind

Whirlwind
    --for my sister, Susan

Ask for that thing
That creates baby sways.
It's yours to hold tight.
Say it creates the folding flower
Scattering between your legs,
The stamen dripping blood,
A yellow center deep within
(The love you're in and making).

Eat honeycombs that are your heart.
There's more than one to nurture.
They're yours to hold tight.
Say there are as many hearts
You care for deep inside
Skipping beats across your whimpers,
Because lying deep within are carved
(Initials of every lover had).

Scatter seeds that bed themselves
In every letter: Birds will come and peck
At lovers still holding tight
And let them go. Cars will stop
To watch the feast and enter into
(This homemade park).

Turn revolutions like a record.
Take stringed instruments, and careful
Kill the notes or hold them tight.
Destroy the heavy bass. Kiss yourself wet.
Close in on your own bent neck.
All the young kisses will unfold down your back.
Envision hands held. Dance that song and bleed
(Deep within).

Stamen and Whirlwind

Say the world is blood and cum.
Race your mind: a red hot car. Make circles,
Hold tight
A self-made placenta. Drown that image
Of what others profess.
Distribute their truth by telling yours,
And in a whirl, what's theirs is gone.
You stay close.
(To hold onto.)
Say balance creates purpose
In the middle of your room: naked, spinning,
(Hold on).

Make out with your shadows
In the city lights: dreams unfold.
Violence disperses. Your tree of life
Is kind to knowing
Your breasts, your womb, your touched birth
Cracking open, pushing out, dropping.
Put yourself back into yourself.
(Each month, a blood creating spins,
A breeze, a whirlwind).

Say that flowers grow from your vagina.
Say raindrops sizzle on your ass.
Say that kisses dream in your heart,
Fill the sun. Say hold your birth soft
(A lifetime).

Say, what happens when tornadoes come?
Those strong swirls/lifts/throwdowns.
Say it's Power
(Like never in your life before).

The Unknown Soldier

You have to be high in some militant way
To go out to any unmarked grave
So full and covered over with
All that graffiti and empty liquor
Bottles. Peace signs plastered
Like an ad or promise; Dark
Like TV or tunnels, and
Such a small statue, hardly someone young,
Or resembling a real person. Faceless.
We might not know; the print on the granite
Says half of what we're to think.
The other half is just old news with some new dirt.

What if we got down on our
Bold hands and knees and dug, dug, dug
Underneath what flowers were left:
American Jim, I wonder if the body would still be there.
Is it (are you) really dead?
Or is it (are you) in some bed sleeping?
A body in an over-filled porcelain tub
Coughing in the secret smoke?

Maybe rhyme awakens bones
After all the skin is gone. Just one eye left trying
To see things hidden, or disappeared.
(Or what a fucked-up childhood...) Pioneers.
That's what humans are. Not Lizard Kings,
Or deliberate chants, but acid and a grave.

Stamen and Whirlwind

Would we after all be caught? Shot excavating one
Last petrified truth? JFK or old-growth trees?
Because it's like them to put back dirt
The way it came,
To padlock fire, offer no lit candles
No sweet incense burning deep to the truth,

While they try to bury our cities
With so many people still in them like mass graves,
Leaving behind large, large abandoned Hotel Morrisons
And calling the leftovers lazy-good-for-nothings.

Stamen and Whirlwind

Trickles
--for Dotson

Spokane mid-morning: soft flakes falling,
Sky gray as a Civil War invasion
Creeps up from the Palouse across the *Safeway* lot.
Reserves are huddled close to loved ones:
Our most precious commodity waiting to be shipped.

This pre-holiday scene fires the imagination.
Our lessons trickle down like tears
Recalling other wars:
The December Wounded Knee Creek Massacre.
Colonel Forsyth and his troops taking Custer's place.
Winter: Contained: All of our ultimate losses
Preserved in stocking salve for after Christmas.
Family tears: the twisted images
Like Bigfoot's body frozen on the Plains.

We gallop into this New Year with lip-synched prayers
As our troops signify a hapless sense of control
Over boundless country that we might
Stretch these holy holidays
Into a stronghold solution for how
We live freely day in and out.

I wonder about Christmas:
How many other past holidays have beefed up our troops,
Have eluded to keep the peace.

Pax Christi Spiritu Sancti: Our young are poised and ready,
Alive in spirited greenery, solid: The very essence
      of flowing river.
Oh River Mighty River Spokane:
      Bless these wheat berry clouds,
The spirits of those 800 shot horses transformed
Forever hooves and manes and shadowy eyes

Stamen and Whirlwind

Trickling down a dark promise lurking from the South
Where heaven and earth are one at the core,
Where water has released itself millions of years over,
Has cooled to rock
Fired up again creating
This High Mass basalt bed we stand free upon.

God Bless the Fruits and Nuts.
God Bless our constant abandonment.
God Bless our independence, frozen in the ground.

Stamen and Whirlwind

Saturday Night Poor Fools
--for brother, Bill

pity those who check the noisy open
doors of bars every one we pass, hoping to
see someone we know or care about
in reckless, smoky air

almost felt like crying to hear that
old beatles tune moaning "yesterday" and
all the troubles snap back on with streetlights
       timed overhead
the empty songs of the black man dancing
across to catch the same bus with his headphones on

pity the ones who watch the night come out
in lonely people the way it is watching
a favorite horse not cross the finish line
the Indian man from some slaughtered tribe
flailing down the aisles of this bus
hoping it will take him somewhere magic, dry and warm
sitting down in everything brown:
the seat his hands his broken leather my country
shoes his face the faded corduroy he wears
falling from his hips slow toward his feet
to make his earth a nice new suit slouched
that tipped taco bell cup empty to the bottom
his dark shadow passing
here falling over this green lake

pity the saturday night fool who sells flowers
at the corner in a wheelchair making circles
in the liquor store parking lot
shouting at customers an incoherent
drunken plea to buy his flowers
and not bottles full of colorless lies
even he knows that love

Stamen and Whirlwind

isn't in there though we've all felt that before
a masked and hidden fear that makes us true
if we touch it

pity the fools attending movies
alone watching writers go crazy on the screen
because no one has the patience
to meet their five personalities

pity the fresh-faced children eating chinese
at the local dragon while this and that one
breathe fire up each others' sleeves picking
the same old thing out on the menu
eating dinner late and to bed early recalling
all those close to them who are dead or dying
for theirs is the kingdom of earth

Stamen and Whirlwind

Reading *Paris Match*

The Natives who say they hate us don't have a slick magazine about it The French parade full-bosomed dreadlocked men between their teeth: Pastel White and Black what a match what a charm mixed with indifference: come out smooth-faced-brown Mama Dig those upper-crusty White men under yellow arches Slicked back money with their sleek Black lucky women See them sprinkle in plazas with their corporate art so fine we cannot touch it Watch this be equated with the Princess who shocks them American Style tastes like French Chic Mama takes her naked dress-up straddled to the knee Disclosed Cowboy Collonus proposing a stronghold transformed from a billboard to Parisian pages depicting American models in satin-stained Kennedy rejects: nothing underneath it leather bomber jackets See Be Happy procreated on a couch draped with red stars and stripes Next page Tragic: Hostage hero without One would not be the French Take dirt-bike-mountain-boot goosesteps with glasses and gun in the hot Haiti sun camouflaging cigarettes from village children's eyes scrambled out unrecognized Misunderstood they stand beside the riot gear It's underwater with the dark blue sector suits and ties meeting two-page worries posing on the steps of ambitious violence *The Match* of course needs men who play good fathers There they are in stripe-clad boxers soaking children in the bathwater Caribbean tattooed with an Indian chief on that whatsoever chest Zapata Viva Viva on a masked horse riding solo against smoking pipes and bullets strapped in X's 'cross their chests No tattoo glamour-soaked up Indians here: Black Mask Eyes Exposed the Zapatistas reflective dark souls are a memory the French need preserve to show how the Other Half Lives...Even in space...Final Frontier before

Stamen and Whirlwind

true discovery Fantasy Stars that cannot scramble or
mix-different made erased exploited chic Pastel White
upon it Like the Cover White-bust bosoms Him holding
onto the darkness of Him holding onto the darkness
That darkness for dear life of dear life for real

Stamen and Whirlwind

Spokane Homecoming
    --for Lynnette

From the antique flow of Prague river
    To your ancestral home, Spokane,
The mighty sparkle of your smile:

        Washington. Water. Power.

Sprinklers full blast in hot basalt summer
    Memories crumble
Unpredictably when you walk on them

    Fountain of the sun, ancient hot language
On the Res of burning sage
    Of times when you were cannon
Exploding outward. Woman mold of Mother
    Breaking force of own sex.
Choices we chose not to discuss,
    Dreams.

Pow-wowing with dancers with drummers.
    On sweetgrass skintight between legs
In disguise as White Columbus.

Hard to be yourself
    Not missing a beaver's beat,
Later swinging to tunes on a quarter.
    Now your hands maneuver
Spokane Falls Boulevard Long Division: Great Divide
    On one way roads you know how to get out
And go without asking.
    Like being swept up
in a wave of revenge,
Released, blown up at the bottom of Upriver Dam.

Stamen and Whirlwind

You twinkle at the base of Minnehaha
Ask pinnacles *How could they tell it was me?*
       Half-moon in sky hovering East
With two clouds surrounding it seems
       I am just that moon
           Half in you Displaced from Seattle, too, while
Other half lingers in shadows yet to be discovered,
       Exhaling camas stars we know are there
But cannot see.   A novel hidden here,
       A lingering ballad that will free.

Gripping your veins: Blue cases, red channels
       Your ridged cheek drinks the milk of moon.

Reincarnation of Peggy Proud
--for Adam Kinsey

*I*n slush he says on the corner of Oak and Pacific, *You're just like her,* recalling his dead Peggy who helped me get through *Ulysses* this quarter: a prayer, each morning a chapter to her soul. *Thank you for your Bloomsday Book, Peggy!* It's 2 am and we're stuffing bits of fresh Fitzbillie's bagels in our mouths grumbling *Fuck, fuck it, fuck that* in a cold sweat potbelly drunk full of too many Bushmills and Cokes and some Buds. We can't even hold our own as he's off on his grandparents: something Kaballah, his 70 year-old father learning Catholicism in Kettle Falls has thrown him off, put him into an *Oh, my god, what god am I from?* state. I'm slowly coming straight out of my buzz thinking, *Friend, you can't figure where you come from anymore, what do you believe in? You say I am like Peggy, then really there's nothing flimsy about me.* It's not like I believe or don't believe in ghosts. Go on and ask now, does that make much sense? Well, *hell no* it doesn't. Take it from the Peggy Part of Me----ghost-like mix of a lot of dead people filling my mouth with pride. There's something truly honorable about being alive as someone who's not present anymore. Feels a lot like being forever an unlocked confessional door. *Oh, I understand* but I don't understand owning and handling, calling the shots, then there's Peggy, and I get that you and her were once knowing how you and I are. Can we shut the backdoor of Spokane Create, a gorgeous swan song for this place without forgetting what a crime it is to be alive not knowing you're dead?

Stamen and Whirlwind

October Wind
--*for Corky Larson (1943-2002)*

*H*eavyweight October Spokane wind
Rabbit punches Bachelor Prairie from the West
Where Channeled Scablands rise and fold,
Disperse terrain jagged as lightning,
New as your being gone.

A crimson flow of emotion half full
Of hope, half undisclosed. I curse
Having to dream up your death.

At this critical stage of season,
Change is falling in our laps.
Gone are long, bright days aboard a boat with
One more intimate word on where to camp.

As you attempt to pop balloons
In your brother's backyard, Pete tries
To replace Dave's screen door. On a Saturday
There were picture-perfect projects: Likely Targets.

Your veins that very evening in collapse
Bridged from one road to the next.

We damn the void. Arrest our souls.
Confine our withdrawal. It is hard to jump
On pain in the presence of the Bagman.

My friend Wylie says in these stretched times
When we wish to erase our own demise
Not call shit on the carpet Blame others
It's easy to point and give up
Our own desire to protect what is precious.

Stamen and Whirlwind

Your life, a pile of leaves that once
Enriched the earth, now blown apart
By obtuse wind.

Stamen and Whirlwind

Letter to Dan Berrigan

dear dan,

today, the blood in the branches has stopped. roofs
have sight. the road, collapsed. squirrels bury their
bodies to protect themselves from the cold coming up to
bite the bark, to bring up the bone, to borrow marrow.
the new baby next door is my alarm clock.
     every morning
i hear her laugh.

right now, there is nothing. goodbye windows
     in empty rooms.
it's single digits out. maybe that's it. here,
     nothing's being
born, only carried in echoes down the ditch to riverbend.
it's flowing chunks of ice stop movement like a red
blood tourniquet. yesterday never showed exactly how
it felt. i'd say numb.

i could drown people crying. i've watched
     "deerhunter" for the
third time. i can't tell. the deer doesn't
     mean much to me. it
used to years ago. depression seems dated. nostalgic.
     not near as
now. can vietnam be dated, dan? the drums, the pain,
the guns rush by, roll over easy.

i used to say my prayers at night, in a rush, rolling fast
when i was five and believed. maybe i need
thanking god the way i once did.
but how can I pray for dreams?

Stamen and Whirlwind

it's bones i'm dreaming up. it's bones blessing the work.
more than ever. what a cracker to miss the ones
       from before,
the dead. to my own bones, i condemn how
disappointment comes and
comes. all the who i am is strangers sitting
       in this uninsulated
spokane house, banging about my head,
       their footsteps hanging
from the ceiling, bodies pounding out the blood.

Stamen and Whirlwind

At the Funeral Home with Mr. Swain

A tape-recorded organ drones. The family has requested six sets of white gloves for the pallbearers to carry Mr. Swain in his fancy cherrywood box to his new home in the ground. Before they put him in, I stare at his closed eyelids, blow his candles out, now alone, putting empty-puddle flower stands back in the flower room. Back there's a place I am so afraid of because it has doors that open and close on their own, doors that swing on wind as though a spirit forces them open for pardon, (tries to keep them from closing, to stop the final light from arriving.) Breathing hard, I enter each viewing room and switch on lamps where cushioned seats have been twisted. Shoved in small spaces are crumpled tissues soggy to the touch which I cautiously pick up so full of crying, bereaved touching someone else's tears: the loss of a self falling down its own still well. It's hauntingly still in the vacant pews where disarmed relatives have just sunken into the shining wood and held still several scents of sweet perfume mixed sick with blessed flowers for Swain. A small child screams in the lobby past the swinging door--like pain--as though it's over Mr. Swain in the form of a fatal final song. Those in attendance proceed to the gates, go black behind wrought iron as I walk out and lock up the way I was taught. Business is business: it protects the world from Truth, the way it keeps the living out to not box them up, up, up too soon, like Mr. Swain, construction worker, who must have looked up at sky and down into basements contemplating heights of life in structured varnish. Back to the office, I shut the organ music off. The crowd drowns out beyond the curb. I stop where I stand to see if I can remember behinds the gates of my eyes, the flower stand behind the door, all the lids closed, held alone. White gloves float like angels, clouds. I flip the switch. Let go of the edge of light, a man, myself.

Bio for Zan Agzigian

Zan was born Sandra Jean Deery in Philadelphia, PA, and moved to the Northwest in 1986. In 1989, she borrowed her mother's maiden name as her nom de plume. She has been in collaboration with Victor A. Charlo co-writing contemporary Native American plays since 1990. Together, they have co-written, directed and produced a number of plays: *Trickster at Dirty Corner, Moon over Mission Dam, The Beta Cycle: Bitterroot, Berkeley, Belfast & Beta*, with *The July: The Whiskey Experience* and *L.A. Christmas Trees* being the most recent.

Zan has devoted many years to arts organizing, and has received grants for fiction, plays, and poetry. Her short story, *White Bees of Winter,* was published in the winter of 2005 in a special First Fiction issue of the Gilcrease Museum's publication, *Gilcrease Journal*.

She lives in Spokane, WA. and works at the BBB *Serving Eastern Washington, North Idaho & Montana* as Communications Director/Lead Fraud Investigator. She regularly reads throughout the NW and performs poetry with musicians under the guise of *Mercury Rising*.